THE HERALDIC ELEPHANT

By

C. Osborn-Jones

*(Master of the Worshipful Company
of Cutlers 1997—1998)*

2015

Published 2015

The Worshipful
Company of
Cutlers

A CIP record for this book is
available from the British
Library

ISBN 978-0-9932459-0-9

Cutlers' Hall
Warwick Lane,
London EC4M 7BR

Printed and bound by CPI Group (UK) Ltd, Croydon, CR0 4YY

CONTENTS

Foreword

Although the elephant has been the symbol of the Worshipful Company of Cutlers for many centuries, its exact origin as our symbol has not been researched in as rigorous a manner as has now been undertaken by Past Master Chris Osborn-Jones.

Elephants are the world's largest land mammals, and one of our most magnificent beasts. A century ago there were over four million animals of at least two species, yet today there are under half a million, as our conflict with them over habitat, and our killing of them for ivory, continues.

Until the middle of the last century, ivory from elephants was extensively used in the manufacture of many products, both decorative and functional. Indeed the word ivory derives from the ancient Egyptian word for elephant. As Cutlers, our use of ivory for the handles of weapons and knives in past times was substantial. This has of course long since ceased, and we now seek to preserve and sustain this endangered animal.

We continue to use our elephant symbol with pride and responsibility, and this important essay explains its significance to our Company and places it in a proper context.

Richard Herbert,

Master of the Worshipful Company of Cutlers, 2014

Acknowledgements

As the research for this little book has taken me in various directions I have received assistance and encouragement from many people and I thank them all. Particular thanks are due to the College of Arms for researching the illustrations of Cutlers' arms and to Philip Lancaster for his encouragement, suggestions and corrections.

Chris Osborn-Jones

Past Master

INTRODUCTION

The City of London is unique in having over one hundred trade guilds known as "Livery Companies" each with its own coat of arms. At Company functions the members wear a badge known as a "livery medal" which has a design usually derived from the Company's arms. The author's livery medal from the Worshipful Company of Cutlers is illustrated on plate i. This was stolen in a burglary and twenty five years later it reappeared on eBay. Since the medal is inscribed with the author's name there was no problem in claiming ownership. The lady who placed the advertisement explained that her late husband had been an amateur dealer and she remembered that years ago he had bought this medal in a job lot. All the other items had been sold on but she had kept this one *because she liked the elephant.* She was now delighted to return it to the rightful owner.

Visitors to Cutlers' Hall in London are always struck by the images of elephants all over the building and want to know how the animal is connected with the Cutlers' Company. This little book is an attempt to answer that question and to explain why it is that, although the animal is not common as a heraldic beast, the icon of the elephant & castle is so widely known today.

This silver denarius was struck to celebrate Caesar's victory in Gaul. In AD 43 the Roman general Claudius invaded Britain with the Praetorian Guard and a phalanx of war elephants. This was the last occasion that a live elephant was seen in this country for more than 1000 years. Yet memory of the animal remained and down the centuries it has been regarded with awe and delight.

The "elephant & castle" as an icon is obviously derived from the fighting elephants of classical times but this does not explain its peculiar popularity from medieval times to the present day. There is a popular tradition that the name is derived from "Infanta de Castile" which was the title of a Spanish princess. There has been little evidence to support this theory and the author of a recent book claims to have "finally laid it to rest".[1] But as I have explored the medieval origins of this heraldic animal, I have come across clues which suggest there may well be truth in this long-established tradition.

2

THE CUTLERS' ELEPHANT

The oldest elephant in Cutlers' Hall is this carved wooden plaque bearing the date 1569 which survived the Great Fire of London. There is some mystery about this item. It was restored in 1908 and only after many layers of paint had been removed was the date revealed so it is surely authentic. But this design was not granted for the Company's arms until 53 years later in 1622.

We need to distinguish between coats of arms and other heraldic devices such as badges and seals. Arms were originally military and armorial designs are always born on a shield. Only these are subject to the laws of heraldry and controlled by the Heralds at the College of Arms. Seals had a civic use in signing legal documents while a badge could be any distinctive mark or design not placed on a shield. The medieval guilds used badges to identify their craft and representations of animals were popular. The Cutlers' 1569 carving is therefore a badge. Badges were often treated as hereditary and it was not uncommon for a design to appear first in a badge or seal and to be later incorporated into a coat of arms.

What is the connection between the Cutlers and elephants? The official records of arms granted in England are held in the College of Arms in London. Heraldic designs often have hidden meanings and pictorial puns on a name are popular but the reasons for the choice of a particular design are not recorded so we can only surmise. King Henry V granted the first charter to the "Commonality of the Mystery of Cutlers" on the 4th December, 1416. Every schoolchild learns how, at the battle of Agincourt, the flower of the French nobility was slain with the aid of the English longbow. But the basic weapon of the infantry was the sword. Since this was the year after Agincourt and the Cutlers' Charter was the only one granted by Henry to a London guild it is reasonable to suppose that it was given in lieu of payment for weapons for his victorious army. The design on the shield of the Cutlers' arms, technically known as the "charge", bears three crossed swords which has an obvious connection with their business but what about the elephant chosen for the crest?

The 14th century saw the spread of plague in Europe with its attendant labour shortages. An act of 1363 had declared that *"no man may take to more than one craft guild"*. The "Commonality of Cutlers" recognised that several separate crafts were to be incorporated into the new Company whose principle trade was manufacture and assembly of finished products. The Charter mentions *"the poverty many in the trade had fallen to through losses at sea"*. How could London cutlers come to suffer losses at sea? Freemen of the Company were at liberty to deal wholesale in commodities related to their trade and this involved importing materials from the continent. Ivory was probably not much in evidence in military weapons but it was an important component for the handles of the quality knives which were a speciality of London cutlers. Records from 1461 confirm that it was being imported in quite large quantities with several references to a "whole tooth" in lists of sales. Imports probably included blades from Germany and other materials used in the manufacture of hilts and scabbards so we can only guess that the animal was chosen because it was already fashionable and held in high regard. City records of 1411 contain a reference to the *"sign of the elephant confirmed for one Simon the leather seller at his premises in Chepe"*. Leather work was the trade of the Scabbarders whose guild was one of those incorporated in the Commonality of Cutlers. Certainly by 1446 the elephant had been adopted by the Company. In civic pageants it was customary for the guilds to have *"conysaunce of every fellowship embroidered on their sleeves"*. The Company's accounts for that year include an entry for the cost of elephants embroidered on the cloaks worn for a civic reception to welcome Queen Margaret for her marriage to Henry VI.[2]

In the early days of heraldry the right to bear arms might be granted by the monarch but it was often assumed or claimed by ancient right of inheritance. Armorial Rolls, which are records of heraldic designs, survive from the 13th century but it was not until the late 14th century that the Court of Chivalry was established to adjudicate in heraldic disputes. It was Henry V who, in 1415, created the office of Garter King of Arms and commanded the Sheriffs *"not to allow any men to bear arms on the forthcoming expedition to France unless by ancestral right or by grant from a competent authority"*. The first Garter King was ordered to accompany the expedition to France on a fee of one shilling a day to ensure this order was carried out.[3] In 1484 the College of Arms took over the role of the Court of Chivalry and during the following century Heraldic Visitations began the task of recording pedigrees and confirming the arms in use throughout England and Wales. Those found to be using arms illegally were stripped of them. A Visitation is often the earliest record of a heraldic design so it is uncertain when it was first adopted. Taxes on the bearing of arms were an additional inducement to avoid official registration.

On the 7th of May, 1476 the 60th anniversary year of its Charter, the Cutlers' Company petitioned for a Grant of Arms which was confirmed by Thomas Holme, Clarencaeux King of Arms. This predates the foundation of the College and the original is lost but details are recorded in the Heraldic Visitation of London of 1568 by Robert Cook, Clarenceaux King of Arms. Visitations by the Heralds were repeated at intervals until the Revolution of 1688. The numerous heraldic manuscripts which survive from the Tudor and Stuart periods include many unofficial copies made for private clients. Official compilations made by the Heralds in the course of their duties are much rarer and it can be difficult to distinguish between an original record and subsequent copies which might incorporate alterations. Cook's Visitation was the source for Volume 1 of the Harleian Society published in 1869. The Society was established to transcribe and publish heraldic manuscripts in the collection begun by Robert Harley 1st Earl of Oxford during the 17th century. The official description of a coat of arms in the technical language of heraldry is called a blazon. On page 6 is the title page and transcription of the Cutlers' blazon from Harley Vol.1.[4]

There are several peculiarities concerning this record. Richard Hawes was not Master of the Cutlers' Company until 1590 so how does this Confirmation of Arms appear in the records of a Visitation made in 1568? Almost all the original records of Visitations are now at the College of Arms. The manuscript records of Cook's 1568 Visitation (MS I G10) seems to be an exception. At this time not all officers of the College deposited their official records in the library as they should, with the result that original manuscripts are sometimes missing. MS I G10 is not the original "office copy" and the working notes of the Visitation are also missing. The official record of 175 folios on vellum (QC MS72) somehow found its way into the library of Queen's College, Oxford and is in Cooke's own handwriting. In 1566 Cook had lodged at the College during a Visitation of Oxford (see page 35). I visited Queen's College to look at these manuscripts but they contain no record of the London Livery Companies. There is evidence of more than one hand in the College of Arms' copy although carefully written to make them appear similar. It must be an "elaborated copy " drawn up later from notes which are now lost.

As an 'improvement' somebody, perhaps a junior herald or scrivener, has added later information including the registration of the London Livery Companies. This would explain the discrepancy of the dates in the Cutlers' entry. [5]

The Visitation of London

In the Year

1568.

TAKEN BY

ROBERT COOKE,

Clarenceux King of Arms,

These be the Armes & crest of Cutlers Incorporated in the fourth yere of the reigne of King Henry the VIth by the name of the Master & Wardens of the Mistrie & Comynaltie of Cutlers of the Citie of London and now regestred in the tyme of the Visitation of London Ao 1590 by Robert Cooke alias Clarenceux King of Armes in the tyme of which Visitation.

Richard Hawes Master, John Gardyner and Thomas Asshott Warden.

*Arms: Gules, three pairs of swords in saltire argent,
the hilts or.
Crest: On a torse argent and gules an elephants
head guls, tusks or.*

The blazon may be accompanied by an illustration but its style will depend on the particular artist. So we find various interpretations of the Cutlers' blazon in early records. The illustration on plate ii, which accompanies the Cutlers' blazon in Harley Vol.1, is from a copy made by Nicholas Charles, Lancaster Herald in 1608. Harley Vol.1 was considered unreliable as the editors could not distinguish between original Visitations and subsequent alterations and it was superseded in 1963 by Harley Vol.109. The illustration on plate iii is now thought to be the earliest interpretation of the Cutlers' blazon. It is from a

6

Visitation of Surrey carried out in 1532 by Thomas Benolt, Clarenceaux King of Arms although the actual illustration was probably done by an assistant.

Thomas Benolt's illustration is very similar in style to the design on the Company's 15th century seal matrix. This would have been necessary for sealing legal documents in the name of the new Company and was probably made soon after the Grant was obtained.

Left: The seal matrix

Right: A wax impression

The illustration on plate iv is from a 16th century armorial in the hand of one Richard Scarlett who was an arms painter and genealogist. The main drawing shows the Cutlers' arms with elephant's head crest but the thumbnail sketch is a design for an elephant & castle. Unlike the 1569 carving in Cutlers' Hall this design has three turrets which was typical of religious images and is thought to have symbolized the Trinity. The scheme is so similar to that on the Great Seal of Coventry that it suggests Scarlett used that city's arms as a model for his design for the Cutlers. (see page 30) The Heralds considered people like Scarlett as a commercial threat and closely guarded their official records. Scarlett died in 1607 so clearly the Company was looking at this new and more fashionable arrangement long before it was authorised. Possibly the Cutlers employed Scarlett to submit a trial design which he included on that page of his armorial.

In 1622 the Company obtained a new Grant of Arms which added a pair of standing elephant supporters and altered the crest to an elephant bearing a castle with two pennants, the left with a red cross and the right with crossed swords which is illustrated on plate v. The thumbnail sketch shows the Cutler' original arms. The new arms were granted by Sir William Segar, Garter King of Arms who in 1613 had been elected a member of the Company.[6] No doubt he advised on the adoption of a more up-to-date design. These arms are recorded in a Visitation of London in 1634 carried out by Sir Richard St George, a long-serving officer of the College of Arms and a noted scholar and antiquary who undertook numerous Visitations. William Segar was Garter King of Arms at the time but Garter did not himself carry out Visitations.

The Visitation of 1634 confirms the original Grant and records the new alterations as follows:

This first Armes & Crest ['*and supporters*' crossed out] *were granted to the Worshipfull Company of the Cutlers by Thomas Holme Clarenceux under the seale of his Armes the 7 of May anno 1486 w*[ch] *said armes and creast were confirmed & approved by Thomas Benolt Clarenceux the 12 of October in the 22 of H:8* [22nd year of reign of Henry VIII, 1531] *in his visitation then made and afterwards confirmed by Robt. Cooke Clarenceux 22 of October 1590.*

Last of all Sir Wm Segar Kt Garter principall king of Armes being a Brother of that Company doth not only confirme the said Coate and alter the Creast but addeth therevnto Supporters in Manner as is aboue depicted by Pattent dated 10 of May 20 of King James [1622].

ffrancis Cobb Master   Joseph Rogers and W[m] **Poulton Wardens.**
Robert   Jadwin   Clarke

Here is another discrepancy. The date of the Cutlers original Grant by Thomas Holme was 1476 not 1486. This is either an office mistake or the Arms may have been confirmed in 1486.[2] Notice that in the illustrations on plates iv and v the helm is missing. Since the helm is an essential part of all arms it was the general custom to omit it in illustrations in trick, that is a sketch with colours indicated by shorthand symbols, whereas full colour illustrations usually did include the helm as in the example on plate iii.

Every heraldic design must be unique but new features can be added to an existing design, a technique known as "differencing". The Cutlers' crest is unusual in that it has a single turret which is round and looks very like a chess castle. We can only guess why this particular design was chosen but its form may owe something to the increasing popularity of the game at that time. The precursor of the modern castle or rook was an elephant with a howdah. The game spread to Europe via Persia and by the 16th century this piece had evolved into its present form but the name "rook" is derived from the Persian word for a war elephant.[7] As the game increased in popularity it became a source of inspiration in art and literature. Poems on the theme of a chess game were fashionable and a particularly famous example had recently been published when the carving in Cutlers' Hall was made.[8]

The illustration below is from "London's Armory" published by Richard Wallace in 1677. This publication includes the Arms of all the London Livery Companies that were active at the time. Like Richard Scarlett, Wallace was an arms painter not a Herald. We do not know what sources he used but he has given the castle a third pennant which has been copied in the Londonderry Guildhall suggesting that Wallace's illustration was used as the model. (see plate vi)

The Cutlers Arms by Richard Wallace. From London's Armory 1677

9

Having obtained a new Grant of Arms with its unusual crest, it is curious that the Cutlers' Company seems then to have ignored the design. The Beadle's head-staff (below left) has an elephant bearing a rectangular castle with four corner turrets. We know little about the provenance of this object although the antique style of the elephant with its flared trunk is reminiscent of earlier religious representations. However the Carrington salt of 1658 (below centre) and the alms box of 1664 (below right) also have rectangular castles. During the 18th century livery medals began to replace the wearing of embroidered gowns. The Cutlers' earliest medal, issued in 1765, is identical to the Author's medal illustrated on plate i. Again the castle is rectangular but it does bear the two pennants of the new Grant of Arms.

The Cutlers of Salisbury

In the refectory of Salisbury cathedral, there is a series of fine Victorian stained glass windows depicting the arms of eight London Livery Companies: Clothmakers, Cordwainers, Cutlers, Goldsmiths, Joiners, Merchant Taylors and Weavers. The Cutlers' window is illustrated on plate vi. The city once had 37 guilds and throughout the 17th and 18th centuries the Cutlers of Salisbury were noted for the excellent quality of their steel products, which was apparently due to some quality of the local water.[9] They had a particular reputation for the manufacture of fine scissors which is commemorated in this ancient rhyme:

> *The height of its steeple,*
> *The pride of its people,*
> *Its scissors and knives*
> *And diligent wives.*

It was the custom to meet the London and Exeter coach and display cutlery to the passengers and it was said to have been "no uncommon thing" to take £70 from a single coach. An 18th century directory includes a reference to "M. Goddard, cutler to their Majestie" and Nell Gwyn is said to have visited the town and to have bought a pair of scissors for 100 guineas. Aubrey wrote that Salisbury was "ever-famous for the manufacture of razors, scissors, and knives". Salisbury cutlers exhibited in the 1851 Great Exhibition but with the rise of industrial manufacturing the guilds went into decline. By 1880 all the Salisbury guilds were defunct however cutlery continued to be produced in the city until the turn of the century. After the demise of the Salisbury cutlers, manufacturers in Sheffield would still use the term "long Salisbury" and "short Salisbury" when referring to table knives and cheese knives.[10]

The windows came from a building in the Market Square constructed in 1878 as a splendid new headquarters for Pinkney's Bank. Oak panelling from the old Weavers' Hall was installed in the public room and stained glass windows specially commissioned to illustrate the work of the most important of the Salisbury Guilds. These windows incorporated the arms of the relevant London Livery Companies. Although the local guilds were by then all defunct the bank's directors felt that association with the London guilds gave it prestige and would encourage trade.[11] The building was largely destroyed in 1976 when Salisbury Town Council redeveloped the area into a shopping precinct. A local refuse collector rescued the badly damaged glass panels from a skip and took them to the works department of the Cathedral. Unfortunately the larger panels showing the work of the guilds were beyond repair but the smaller panels with the arms of the London guilds were installed in the new refectory.

The Company of Cutlers in Hallamshire

The historic district known as Hallamshire encompasses a number of parishes centred around Sheffield. As early as the 14th century the area was noted for the production of knives. The trade was supervised by the Lord of the Manor through the Manorial Courts which also issued marks. Sheffield cutlers were keen to emulate their London brethren and there are records of the London dagger mark being used on their wares. As the trade developed in importance the need arose for better control and Parliament was petitioned for an Act of Incorporation. The Cutlers Company of London did not oppose the Bill but it did raise concerns about the counterfeit use of London marks.

11

It had been common custom for provincial guilds to use the arms of the equivalent London company. In 1624 The Company of Cutlers in Hallamshire was incorporated. Having no official arms of its own, the new Company adopted the old arms of the London Cutlers. These were placed above the entrance of its first hall and continue to adorn the present hall. The Company's accounts record the cost of a painting of the arms displayed in their first hall when it opened in 1638 but the earliest surviving example, dated 1692, comes from the chimney breast of a house believed to have been occupied by one Tobias Ellis who became Master of the Company in 1718. It was rescued when the house was demolished and installed in the Hall. Before the Company built its first hall it reputedly held its meetings in a public house called the "Cutlers Inn" in Fargate.[12] Although no surviving records are able to verify that they definitely used this building, its existence is confirmed on a street map dated 1806 and it was located just adjacent to where the Cutlers built their hall.[13] A contemporary sketch shows the form of the arms on the inn sign. It is based on those of the London Company with an interesting variation. The shield has three short swords or daggers in place of crossed swords. The Company also borrowed the motto "*Pour parvenir a bonne foy*" from the London cutlers, although spelt slightly differently, and this can be seen on the tiled floor of the entrance hall.

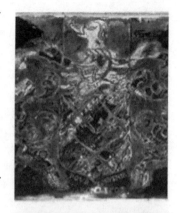

Top: *Chimney breast of Tobias Ellis*
Centre: *The Cutlers Inn in Fargate*
Bottom: *Arms above the entrance of the present Cutlers' Hall*

It is a nice irony that in more recent times the Hallamshire Company was concerned about the counterfeit use of its marks and the name 'Sheffield' on inferior foreign made goods. After the Trade Marks Registration Act was passed in 1875 the Sheffield Advisory Committee was set up to investigate infringements. And when the British Empire League proposed the recognition of an Empire Trade Mark, the Company objected.

The Company of Cutlers in Hallamshire received its own Grant of Arms in 1875. The new Grant differenced the crest with crossed swords and the charge with sheaves of arrows and corn on a green field. This is derived from the arms of Sheffield city and is a pun on the name of the river "Sheaf" and "field". In heraldic terms this is known as a rebus. The arms of the Hallamshire and London Companies are depicted in a pair of stained glass windows in the Cutlers' Hall in Sheffield, which are illustrated on plate vi. The designer of the windows was obviously confused about the subtle differences between these arms. In the London arms the crest of 1476 has mistakenly been combined with the supporters from the arms of 1622. In the Sheffield arms the London spelling of the motto has been used instead of the correct Sheffield variation which should be:

"Pour Y Parvenir a Bonne Foi "

Londonderry Guildhall

The Plantations of Ulster in the reign of James I were largely financed with cash extracted under duress from the London guilds. These were organised into syndicates led by the wealthiest guilds and the Cutlers were included in the Salters' Company Syndicate.. By the end of the 19th century all the Livery Syndicates had sold their interest in the Irish estates but the Honourable Irish Society continues to play an important charitable role in the region.

The original Guildhall in Londonderry was built to commemorate the role of the London Guilds in the founding of the city. The present building, which dates from 1890, was paid for by the Honourable Irish Society and contains a fine series of stained glass windows depicting the arms of the Livery Companies in the Irish syndicates. The hall was virtually destroyed during the troubles but the windows have been recreated from the original designs. The Cutlers' window is also illustrated on plate vi. The form of the castle with its third pennant suggests that Richard Wallace's illustration was used as the source.

THE ELEPHANT & CASTLE OF NEWINGTON

The Elephant & Castle district of Newington in South London is derived from a famous coaching inn on the site where several roads met, leading to Kent and Surrey. Before the coming of the railway the location would have been familiar to any traveller going South. The earliest record of the name is in the Court Leet Book of the Manor of Walworth which records that it met at The Elephant & Castle, Newington on 21st of March, 1765. In its Victorian heyday Newington, which was on the tram line and the electric railway, became famous for its department stores, music halls and the Theatre Royal. When this burnt down in 1878 it was rebuilt as the Elephant & Castle Theatre which indicates that the name was already in general use.

The area was severely damaged in the Blitz suffering one of its worst tragedies when a bomb penetrated the tube station where hundreds of people were sheltering. It was redeveloped in the 1960s becoming one of London's busiest traffic intersections. Few areas are so linked with post-war modernism. The neo-brutalist Heygate Estate, conceived as an icon of Corbusian social architecture, became the focus of various controversies. One way and another it is probably the Elephant & Castle of Newington that has been most influential in making the name so well known.

Top: Photograph by Bert Hardy, Picture Post magazine - 1949
Bottom: The Elephant & Castle Theatre

Most recent references to the area go back to Walford's "Old and New London" which states simply that the Elephant & Castle inn at Newington was so named because its sign was the crest of the Cutlers' Company.[14] It has long been a traditional name for public houses in England but Walford does not explain how this inn came to be associated with the Cutlers' arms. In 1641 one John Flaxman sought permission of the Vestry Council to set up a blacksmith's shop at the cross roads where the business would gain trade from the passing traffic. He was succeeded by various lease holders who extended the business and for some years the property was known as the White Horse.[15]

In 1751, after the opening of Westminster Bridge, the Turnpike Trust upgraded the road and a coaching inn was built on the site. This was apparently a time when the Cutlers' Company was trying to tighten its control over the trade for in 1756 it obtained an Act of Common Council which forbade all but members of the Company to be employed as cutlers. It seems likely that the business had diversified into cutlery and was now trading under the sign of the Elephant & Castle. The northern part of Southwark was technically within the City until 1900 and, although the village of Newington was just outside, several Livery Companies were active in the area. The Drapers and the Fishmongers still have alms houses there. At the time of this illustration the dwelling next door was occupied by Joanna Southcott, a religious prophetess, and the locality was the focus of a considerable movement of followers known as Southcottians.

The old Elephant & Castle in 1818
Joanna Southcott lived in the house
on the right

There had been some association with the elephant in this area of South London from an earlier date. The "Elephant Stairs" are a flight

15

of Watermen's steps on the Southwark bank first recorded on John Stow's map of 1598.[16] In Shakespeare's play "Twelfth Night", first performed in 1601, Antonio says *"In the south suburbs, at the Elephant, is best to lodge"*. Although the play is set in a foreign land, Shakespeare often used local London references and the theatres were all located in this area. At the beginning of the 17th century there was a theatre in Newington parish which was home to a company of players called the "Lord Admiral's and Lord Chamberlain's Servants" and this theatre was sometimes used by the players from the Globe.

In 1661 there was a curious report of a vision seen in the clouds from London Bridge involving an elephant & castle.[17] The event was recorded in a pamphlet with the grand title:

"Strange News from the West, being Sights seen in the Air Westward, on Thursday last, being the 21st day of the present March by divers persons of credit standing on London Bridge between 7 and 8 of the clock at night."

Although this was an age for seeing wonders in the air the credulous observers must have been familiar with the icon. Perhaps it was also a premonition for, when Old London Bridge was demolished in 1831 and its materials sold, a cutler in the Strand bought 15 tons of the iron that had shod the piers and declared that it made the best steel for knives.[18]

Another curious little example of the icon continuing in the common vernacular occurred when George I came to London in 1714 and brought his two mistresses with him. Neither George nor the mistresses were at all popular with the common people in London. The tall thin mistress was contemptuously known as the "Bean Pole" while Sophia Von Kielmansegg who was apparently fat and ugly was called the "Elephant & Castle". [19]

MEDIEVAL ELEPHANTS

To understand better the Cutlers' choice of an elephant for their arms it will help to delve further into the history of pachyderm iconography. The animal was popular throughout the medieval period and numerous representations are found in illustrated manuscripts and ecclesiastical carvings. The Cutlers' 1476 crest clearly owes more to these than to any first hand knowledge of the animal. Bestiaries are collections of animal stories illustrating events from the bible. Medieval bestiary manuscripts were often beautifully illustrated, the pictures serving as a visual language for the illiterate public. It was believed that the natural world had been created by God as a source of instruction for humanity. God gave each animal particular characteristics to serve as examples for proper conduct and to reinforce the teachings of the Bible. Anatomical details of the animals are often imaginative, faithfully reproducing misconceptions in earlier versions. One of the oldest surviving bestiaries is the *Hexameron* which was composed by Saint Ambrose, Bishop of Milan, in the 4th Century. This contains a treatise on the elephant which includes a description of the trunk emerging from the top of the animal's head and describes how the female gives birth in water to protect her young from her only foe, the dragon.

Above: The trunk emerging from the top of the animals' head.
C14th Bavarian ms. - Bibliothèque Nationale de France

Below: A female giving birth to her young in water.
C13th English codex - Bodleian Library

It was also believed that elephants lacked knee joints so were unable to lie down and if one fell over it would be unable to get up. They therefore slept leaning against a tree. In the bestiary story, while an elephant is sleeping, a hunter cuts down the tree and the animal falls helplessly to the ground. Unable to rise it cries out. Other elephants try but are unable to help it. Finally an infant elephant succeeds in raising the Fallen One with its trunk. The story illustrated the medieval concept of the Fall and Redemption through the power of the tree or cross.

The elephant leans against a tree that   A baby elephant raises the
has been cut by a hunter.   Fallen One.
C13 "Bestiaire d'Amour"   Bestiary of Guillaume le Clerc"
- Bibliothèque Nationale de France

Being such a mighty beast, the only foe of the elephant was the dragon. The Great Elephant and his wife represented Adam and Eve who also had their dragon in the form of the Tempter in the Garden of Eden.[20] We also find the elephant, the tree and the dragon together in early heraldic form in the 14th century Great Seal of Coventry. (see page 30)

The elephant is attacked by   The elephant tramples
a dragon.   the dragon
Bestiaire d'Amour - MS O.2.14 Trinity College

The Great Elephant and his wife with Adam and Eve in the Garden of Eden are warned not to eat the forbidden fruit.

"Bestiary of Guillaume le Clerc" - Bibliothèque Nationale de France

The following extracts are from the 13th century Bestiary of Guillaume le Clerc. The original is in Latin in rhyming verse. They describe the moral virtues of the elephant and how they give birth to their young in water. It also illustrates the way in which biblical stories were conflated with historical events. [21]

We ought not to hold the story of the elephant up to mockery;
It is the biggest beast there is and will carry the greatest burdens.
It is full wise and understanding and in battle very useful.
The Indians and the Persians when they go to war
Are wont to load great towers on it,
There mount up the archers and the knights.
It is a wise beast and does not often breed;
When the time comes that it will beget young,
Then it goes to the East and takes its female with it
To paradise where man was first placed.
She fears the dragon so much that in a pond she goes to give birth,
To keep her young from death and the male waits outside
To guard and defend them both.
In these two beasts truly are Eve and Adam figured.
When they were in paradise set in plenty and in joy,
They did not know what evil was.

19

This strange depiction of an elephant & castle is from a 13th century Icelandic manuscript. It illustrates how widespread was familiarity with the icon even in a country that clearly had never been visited by an elephant. The animal's great size and strength is described and how, in battle, it can carry a castle constructed of wood. In this manuscript the story is conflated with the Old Testament Book of Maccabees. This seems curious but, in 1235, the King of Jerusalem, John de Brienne, who had adopted the elephant & castle

MS 673A - University Library of Copenhagen

as a personal badge, won a great victory that was lauded throughout Christendom by chroniclers, who compared his feat to classical champions including the heroes of the Maccabees. (see page 26)

Norman masons would certainly have been familiar with the symbolism associated with animals in the bestiary stories. There are 12th century examples of their work that have clearly been inspired by bestiary illustrations although these are rare and have often been damaged by iconoclasts who considered them idolatry. The illustrations below show the great fight between Draco and the elephant.

Right: C15th misericord , Carlisle cathedral

Left: C12th font. Dunkeswell church, Devon.

20

The medieval French village of Aulnay de Saintonge lay on an important pilgrimage route. The church of St. Peter dates from 1140, in the south aisle there is a capital with three elephants bearing a helpful Latin inscription explaining "Here are elephants". The unusual accuracy of their anatomy  suggests that the sculptor had first-hand knowledge of the animal.

During the 13th and 14th centuries there was a flourishing of decorative carving in English church furniture which shows increasing heraldic influence.[22] The elephant & castle was a popular theme and there are many fine examples in churches and cathedrals. The quality and position of these carvings indicates the high status in which the icon was regarded.

poppy head
- All Saints church
Willian, Herts

bench head
- C14th choir stalls
Chester cathedral

misericord
- St. George's chapel
Windsor

In Ripon cathedral there is a magnificent example of a carved elephant & castle on the bishop's throne. Ripon was the seat of a bishop for a short period in St Wilfrid's time but the modern diocese was only constituted in 1836. Before this Ripon was a Collegiate Church and the throne would have been occupied by the Archbishops of York. The decoration of the throne includes a mitre and the shield of St Wilfrid supported by two angels bearing a scroll with the date 1494. The carving probably has no heraldic significance. The elephant is facing a smaller carving of a defeated Greek centaur so the arrangement may be an allegorical allusion to the classical wars

21

between the Persians and the Greeks in which the Persian use of elephants gave them an important military advantage. The castle, with its defenders peering over the parapet, is very similar in style to the one on Viscount Beaumont's memorial and only a few years separate the two. (see page 28)

Abul-Abbas was an elephant given to the Emperor Charlemagne by the caliph of Baghdad in AD 797. The elephant's name and events from his life are recorded in the Annales Regni Francorum (Annals of the Kingdom of the Franks). Some sources state that Abul-Abbas was an albino. Charlemagne took Abul-Abbas with him on his campaign against the Danes in AD 804 although the animal was not actually involved in the fighting.

Above: Bishop's throne, Rippon cathedral. The carving is only about six inches in height.
Below: C12 fresco of an albino war elephant- San Baudelio

The Cremona Elephant was a gift from Sultan Al-Kamul of Egypt to Holy Roman Emperor Frederick II in 1229. The elephant took part in Frederick's triumphal parades and the event was recorded by Matthew Paris, the Chronicler of St. Albans. This was the first elephant to be reported from first-hand experience since Abul-Abbas.

The Author's Livery medal from the Worshipful Company of Cutlers.

Ivory traders. From a window in Cutlers' Hall

plate i

ℭutlers

Ghese be the Armes and Creast of Cutlers Incorprated in
the fourth yere of the reigne of Kinge henry the vjth by the
name of master and wardens of the mistrie and Comynaltie
of Cutlers of the Citie of London: And now regestred in the
tyme of the visitacion of London A 1590 by Robert Cooke alias
Clarencieulx Kinge of Armes / in the tyme of which visitation
Richard hawes was master, John Gardyner and Thomas
Asshott wardens :

*The Cutlers' Arms from Harley Vol.1 by Nicholas
Charles 1608*

College of Arms manuscript 1 G10 f22

plate ii

*The Cutlers' Arms from Thomas Bemolt's Visitation of Surrey
1532*

College of Arms manuscript 1 H7 f59

plate iii

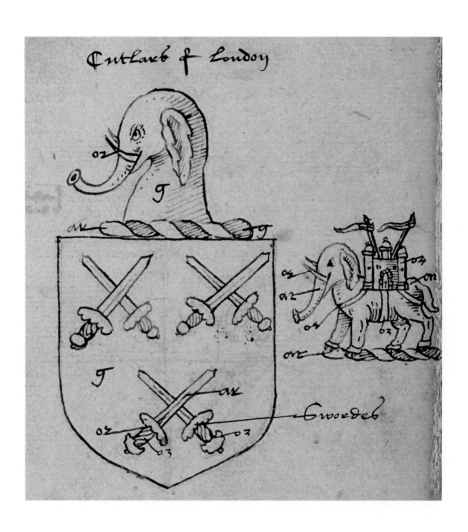

The Cutlers' Arms from Richard Scarlet with a design for an elephant & castle

College of Arms manuscript Vincent 183 f4a

plate iv

The Cutlers' Arms from Richard St George, Visitation of
London 1634 - College of Arms manuscript 2C 24 f199

plate v

Windows in the Cutlers' Hall in Sheffield.
Left: the Sheffield Company's 1875 arms with differencing;
Right: the London Company's arms.

Left: *The Cutlers' window in Londonderry Guildhall*
Right: *Cutlers' window from Pinkney's Bank, Salisbury*

plate vi

The King's Elephant is the earliest recorded visit of an elephant to this country. It was presented by Louis of France to King Henry III in 1255 and was kept in the Royal Menagerie at the Tower of London where it lived for four years. The text below the illustration states that its keeper was named Henry of Florence.[23] The elephant was already associated in

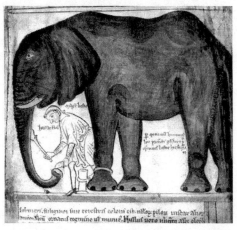

the public's mind with the religious stories and the arrival of this animal must have been a wondrous event. Matthew Paris recorded the occasion in his *Chronica Majora* and noted that people flocked to see it. The Royal Menagerie remained in the Tower until 1834 when it was transferred to Regents Park and the Zoological Society of London was founded.

- Chronica Majora MS Parker 16 Corpus Christi College

During the 13th century, travellers to Asia began to bring back reports of fighting elephants. Such accounts are often distorted by contemporary moralizations from the bestiaries. In this page from "The Travels of Marco Polo" the elephant with its flared trunk is typical of bestiary illustrations.

TRANSITION TO HERALDRY

The examples below demonstrate transition from military to heraldic form of the castle. On the left it is a wooden platform with Persian soldiers. On the right it has become a castellated Norman tower.

Anne Walsh bestiary   C13 bronze candlestick   C13 French bestiary
Konelige Biliotek   Victoria & Albert Museum   MS Parker 53

The illustration on the next page is from one of the most famous early renaissance combat manuals by the master of swordsmanship Fiore Dei Liberi, published in manuscript form around 1409. In this section he is describing the qualities a successful swordsman must seek. The diagram shows the various sword strokes and explains the attributes each requires, illustrating the point with an appropriate heraldic beast. The elephant is not associated with an individual stroke but rather represents the strength and fortitude which must underpin the entire swordsman's skill. The text above the elephant translates as follows:

I am the elephant and I have a castle for a burden and never do I kneel down nor do I lose my burden .

This is neither a bestiary nor a heraldic representation but it well illustrates the contemporary popularity of the icon and the high regard in which it was held.

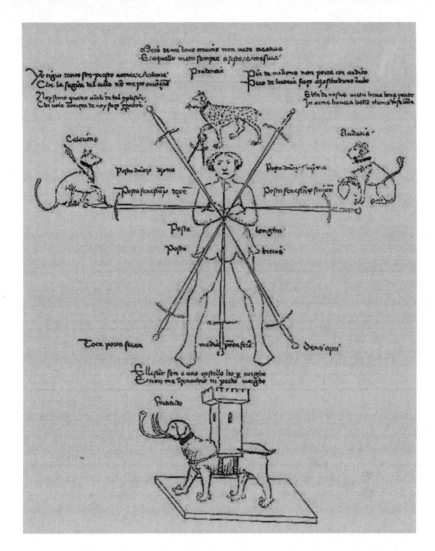

As the science of heraldry developed many bestiary animals were adopted into new coats of arms. As a heraldic symbol the elephant denoted strength and wisdom and, as the bearer of royalty, power while the castle signified security. The heraldic treatise of Sir William Comings, Lyon King of Arms dated 1494 contains a symbolic interpretation which is roughly translated as follows: [25]

The elephant has teeth of ivory and has growing tusks and among all the other beasts he is master of body and virtue and of good memory. And in his deeds in water and on land he is protected by his size. He is born of long life and, of all beasts, his generation is worthy of memory.

THE INFANTA DE CASTILE & THE BEAUMONTS

There is a long-standing tradition that the name "Elephant & Castle" is derived from "Infanta de Castile". The Infanta was the eldest daughter of a Spanish king without a claim to the throne. Two years before acceding to the English throne in 1625, Charles I made an incognito visit to Castile in an attempt to conclude a marriage treaty with the Infanta. The mission failed because Charles refused conversion to Roman Catholicism, a condition imposed by the Spanish government. This romantic setback so angered the young prince that it helped to trigger war against Spain a few months later. It is supposed that the eponymous inn at Newington was named to mark his journey on the route out of London to Dover. There is absolutely no evidence to support this theory. However the association of the Infanta with the elephant & castle may go back to the very beginning of heraldry.

Queen Eleanor, first wife of the Plantagenet King Edward I, was an Infanta de Castile. She was the eldest daughter of Ferdinand III, king of Leon and Castile. Eleanor and Edward were devoted to each other and she accompanied him on all his military campaigns. Jerusalem had fallen in 1244. In 1270 Edward and Eleanor joined the 9th Crusade with 200 knights and 1000 men to relieve the city of Acra. They were away for four years and during this time Eleanor bore three of their numerous children. Such an extraordinary example of domestic harmony in the midst of a military campaign must have made a special impression on their followers. It has been suggested that the returning crusaders used the sobriquet "Elephant & Castle" to refer to Queen Eleanor.

Queen Eleanor was the grand daughter of John de Brienne, King of Jerusalem, and his third wife the Infanta Berenguela of Castile and Leon whose arms were a lion and a three towered castle. In one of the most remarkable careers of the medieval period, John de Brienne rose from the rank of a middle class knight to become King of Jerusalem and Emperor of Constantinople. In 1235 he repelled a siege of the city in a famous victory which was widely celebrated by contemporary chroniclers.[26] De Brienne had adopted the elephant & castle as a badge.[27] Heralds often attributed devices to characters from ancient times and these are known as "preheraldic arms". The elephant was considered to be a symbol for royalty in Biblical times and the elephant & castle is thought to have been regarded as an emblem for the Kingdom of Jerusalem.[28] Surely the crusader knights who were with Edward and Eleanor at Acra would have been aware of Eleanor's descent from her famous crusader ancestor?

It is now difficult to distinguish fact from fiction in the traditions associated with Queen Eleanor. Her popular image owes much to the writings of the 16th century antiquary William Cambden who interpreted the events of three hundred years earlier in the light of his own, very different, post-reformation perspective. Cambden's accounts were often repeated by later historians without reference to original sources so that by the time the Victorian author Agnes Stickland came to write her great work on "The Lives of the Queens of England" the account of Eleanor's life had become embellished with 19th century romanticism.[29] Eleanor died in 1290 on the way to join Edward who was campaigning in Scotland and her mourning husband erected crosses at the twelve places where her funeral cortege halted on its journey back to Westminster. Only three of these now survive but so strong was the Victorian fascination with Queen Eleanor that in 1864 the directors of the South Eastern Railway Company decided to name their new terminus "Charing Cross Station" and built a replica of the cross that had been erected nearby 574 years previously.

In St. Mary's church Wivenhoe, in Essex, there is a fine memorial brass to William Viscount Beaumont who died in 1507 and his wife Elizabeth Scrope, daughter of Sir Richard, 1st Baron Scrope of Bolton. Viscount Beaumont is dressed in full Tudor armour with his feet resting on an elephant bearing a castle from which three armed men peer. The broom pod beneath his feet indicates the family's relationship to the Plantagenet dynasty. The spandrels are decorated with more elephants & castles. Viscount Beaumont was a leader on the Lancastrian side during the Wars of the Roses and he spent his final years under the care of his former comrade at arms John de Vere, Earl of Oxford, on the Earl's estate at Wivenhoe. The brass in St Mary's church was instructed by his widow Elizabeth who later married De Vere but chose to be buried next to her first husband in Wivenhoe.

It *is* only a coincidence but such a curious one that I cannot resist mentioning it here. It was Sir Richard Scrope, 1st Baron Bolton, who built Bolton Castle in Yorkshire where, in 1568, Mary Queen of Scots was imprisoned under the guardianship of Henry Scrope 9th Baron.

While there, Mary was tutored in English by Sir Francis Knollys, Knight for the Shire of Oxford. Subsequently both Bolton in Lancashire and the City of Oxford adopted an elephant in their arms. (see page 36 and 40)

One of the spandrels

Enlargement of the castle

Viscount William Beaumont traced his ancestry back to John de Brienne. Naturally the family would want to demonstrate their relationship to such an illustrious ancestor. The elephant & castle was adopted by this branch of the Beaumont family in recognition of their descent from John de Brienne. As the grand daughter of John de Brienne, Queen Eleanor was closely related to the Beaumonts. John De Brienne's son Louis d'Acre married Agnes Vicomtesse de Beaumont and assumed the Beaumont name. His grandson Henry de Beaumont, and Queen Eleanor were thus cousins. Henry served both Edward I and Edward II in the Scottish wars where he pioneered the tactics which were later used so successfully at Crecy and Agincourt. As a reward he was created 1st Baron Beaumont by Edward II who designated him as "the King's kinsman" in recognition of their consanguinity through Queen Eleanor.[30]

The great Cloisters of Canterbury Cathedral were built around 1400 and the roof bosses are decorated with the arms of the various benefactors. One of these bosses has an elephant bearing a castle that is transitional between bestiary and heraldic representations. The elephant is not placed on a shield but bears the shield as part of the harness for the castle. The harness bands can be seen  running forwards and backwards from the shield which bears the arms of Jerusalem. This boss is surrounded by the arms of the various branches of the Beaumont family.

In 1327 Baron Beaumont was granted the estate of Beaumanor in Charnwood Forest, Leicestershire. Here he built a manor house and a chapel named St. Mary in the Elms which was consecrated in 1338. Six generations of Beaumonts followed. In 1450 John Beaumont installed a remarkable series of heraldic windows in the chapel illustrating the arms of the various branches of the family, their allies and allegiances.[31] When William Viscount Beaumont was buried at Wivenhoe he was without issue and in 1595 the estate passed to the Herrick family.

The Beaumont chapel is now the parish church of Woodhouse. Sadly nearly all of the medieval glass was lost during a Victorian restoration but fortunately we have a detailed description.[32] Here again were to be found the elephant bearing a castle both in the windows and carved in the end post of the pews. The arms of Jerusalem were also represented in the windows.

Sketch of a bench end in Woodhouse chapel.
From Leics.Architect. and Archaeol. Soc. Vol I July 27th 1859

All Saints Parish Church in Loughborough was once part of the Beaumont estate and, during the 15th century, the Beaumont family were Lords of the Manor of Loughborough. The roof of the nave has a fine series of 65 gilded bosses. Among these is another representation of the Beaumont elephant & castle.

Coventry appears to be the earliest use of the elephant & castle as a specifically heraldic device. The right to use arms was probably conferred when Eleanor's grandson Edward III granted the first charter of incorporation to the city in 1345. The arms are based on the "Sigillum Coventrae" or Great Seal which was found to be in use at the time of the first Heraldic Visitation in 1540. This was described as showing an elephant standing by two trees, bearing on its back a castle with three golden domes; the reverse showing the combat between the Archangel Michael and the dragon. The illustration below was based on a later Visitation. [33] There is good reason to believe that it is the original seal of the city and probably the one recorded in the 1540 Visitation. It is from a two-sided wax impression appended to the tail of a document dated 1349.

The

Visitation of Warwickshire,

1682-1683.

Coventry.

Richard Scarlet's design for the Cutlers' Company

The White Seal for Certificates etc.

The great Seal of the Cittie to Seal Deeds etc.

The Ring Seal for Letters etc.

Several suggestions have been put forward as to how the city came to adopt the elephant & castle and they may all have had some degree of influence. Coventry was an important centre of the wool trade and the elephant may have its origin as a mark for woollens exported to the Levant.

The early trade guilds were religious fraternities and this is often reflected in their emblems. The wool trade in Coventry was represented by the "Shearmen and Fulers of the Guild of Nativity of our Lord of Coventry". There is an obvious connection with the bestiary story where the tree, the elephant and the dragon appear together. The tree is also associated with the city's name. An early form of Coventry is "Cofantreo" which was Saxon for "Coffa's tree".[34] The arms of the Comb Makers, a long extinct London Livery Company, also had a crest with an elephant leaning against a tree. Like the Cutlers, their trade involved the use of ivory. The most intriguing link with the elephant & castle is the close association of the city and its arms to the family of Eleanor of Castile. It is easy to understand how, after the disastrous reign of Edward II, a device that recalled his illustrious mother, the Infanta de Castile, would have been a happy choice.

Above Left: Comb Makers' crest

Above Centre: The modern civic arms of Coventry city. The supporters are a recent addition. Note that the two trees have now disappeared. The crest bears a wild cat. Compare this with the thumbnail of the lion gardant from the crest of Edward the Black Prince on the right.

In addition to its charter, there are several other links associating the city with the Plantagenet royal family. Edward II was born at Caernarfon Castle in 1301 and was presented to the Welsh people as the first Prince of Wales. His grandson Edward the Black Prince was Lord of the Manor of Cheylesmore in Coventry which is remembered in the city's motto "Camera Principis" (Prince's Chamber) and on the flag above the tower on the Great Seal is the Prince of Wales's feathers which he introduced.

At the Visitation of 1540 the city's crest was described as a cat-a-mountaine. But the earliest refercnce to this animal as a heraldic beast is in connection with an entirely different Black Prince, the prince of Monomotapa, a 15th century African kingdom that had recently been discovered by the Portuguese as they explored along the coast of that continent.[35] How could this animal have been adopted in the arms of the city at its incorporation in 1345? The crest of Edward the Black Prince was a lion gardant. In heraldry the lion gardant is also called a leopard while the wild cat is sometimes described as a mountain lion.[36] Comparing the illustration of Edward's crest with that on the Coventry civic arms on the previous page it is easy to see how the two could be confused. At the Visitation the crest could easily have been wrongly identified by the Heralds so possibly Coventry inherited not only its motto but also its crest from Edward the Black Prince.

The Statute Seal of the city bears Edward III's head between two Plantagenet broom pods whose arrangement is reminiscent of the trees on the Great Seal. The portrait is clearly based on the coin portrait of Edward's reign. Beneath is a lion gardant from his royal arms.[37]

Left:
City of Coventry
Statute Seal

Right:
Edward III
silver groat

PWLLHELI AND THE MADRYN SEAL

The town of Pwllheli in the county of Gwynedd has no arms but it possesses a seal depicting an elephant bearing a three towered castle standing by two trees. It has the following inscription: *"Sigillum communitatis ville de Porthely"* This seal is the basis for the logo adopted by Pwllheli Council. The first account of the seal appeared in a publication of 1913 where it was described as "probably dating from 1422 when the town's charter was confirmed by Henry VI".[38] There was no noble family associated with the town or any other local borough that could have possessed these arms so what could the connection be?

The seal was apparently discovered in 1857 at "Madryn", an old mansion on the outskirts of Pwllheli, by the owner Mr. Jones Parry who presented it to the council. It subsequently emerged that Mr. Parry had not actually discovered the seal but had had it made according to his recollection of an old design although he was unable to provide documentary evidence for this. The date 1857 is significant for the town council had just been revived after lying dormant for several years and the discovery of an ancient seal would have provided a welcome boost to civic pride. The Town Clerk, who had been closely involved in the endeavour to establish the municipal status, had resigned the previous year and it transpired that he was related to Mr. Jones Parry.[39]

Left: The Madryn seal

Right: The logo of Pwllheli Council

The Council had previously used a seal with a goat rampant but this had fallen into disuse and been lost. When it was rediscovered in 1905 it was noticed that the inscription on this seal was exactly the same as that on the Madryn seal. The Madryn seal is typically 15th century in style but both its close resemblance to the Coventry seals and the circumstances surrounding its discovery lead to the conclusion that it was a fabrication. But why should a small town in Wales wish to emulate the arms of an English City 150 miles away? Pwllheli is just a few miles from Caernarfon and it was Edward the Black Prince who in 1355 gave the town its first Charter as a free borough. It seems probable that Mr Jones Parry and the Town Clerk were aware of the historical connection between Pwllheli, Caernarfon and Coventry City and sought to make use of it to enhance the status of the Council.

THE FASHIONABLE ELEPHANT

After the adoption of the heraldic device by Coventry, the elephant & castle became established as a fashionable icon and we find a number of great families using it. Each example has an interesting story to tell.

THE VERNON FAMILY

Saint Bartholomew's church at Tong in Shropshire is famous for its collection of memorials to the Vernon family. There is a fine brass to Sir Henry Vernon and his widow Margaret in which the lady's feet rest on an elephant & castle in a manner very similar to the Beaumont memorial. Although the castle cannot be seen, the belly bands on the elephant are visible. It has been suggested that the elephant is a rebus on Lady Vernon's name saint Margaret who was attacked by a dragon, thus linking it to the bestiary story.[40] The date of this bronze is 1467, just nine years earlier than the Cutlers' first grant and the similarity of the elephants with ribbed ears is striking. Note also the two sets of tusks.

SIR ROBERT ONLEY

Sir Robert Onley was a prosperous wool merchant who lived in Coventry, twice becoming mayor in the 1480s. He was buried in 1512 in Withington church in Shropshire. The memorial, ordered by his son John Onley, has adopted the elephant with a triple towered castle from the arms of Coventry city although the castle is highly elaborated. The animal also possesses clearly ribbed ears.

Left: Vernon family   *Right: Robert Onley*

SIR ROGER CORBET

Arms with a crest of an elephant & castle were granted to Sir Roger Corbet, High Sheriff of Shropshire, in 1529. Here the castle is a single turret very similar in style to that on the Cutlers' 1569 plaque. The tomb of Sir Roger and his wife, who was also named Margaret, is in the church of Saint Bartholomew in Morton Corbet. It is covered in heraldry and you need to look carefully to spot the elephants alternating with owls beneath the shields. [41]

THE KNOLLYS FAMILY AND OXFORD CITY

These are illustrated on the next page. Sir Thomas Knollys was a member of the Grocers Company and Lord Mayor of London who, in 1400, directed the rebuilding of the Guildhall. The crest of the Knollys family arms is a silver elephant. The arms of Oxford were first recorded in a Visitation of 1566 by Robert Cooke who also carried out the London Visitation. Cooke lodged at Queens College during the Visitation. Also present was:

"Sr Francis Knowlles Treasurer of the Quennes Majestie's household & one of her Majestie's most honourable privie Counsaill, Stewarde of the said cittie and towne". [42]

Sir Francis was a descendant of Sir Thomas Knollys. The elephant supporter in the city arms was confirmed in 1574 by Richard Lee, Deputy to Robert Cooke.

Sir Francis was a descendant of Sir Thomas Knollys. The elephant supporter in the city arms was confirmed in 1574 by Richard Lee, Deputy to Robert Cooke.

Left: Arms of the Knollys family   *Right: Arms of Oxford City*

ROSSEND CASTLE

Clan Oliphant is derived from a Norman family that was granted lands in Scotland during the 12th century. Perversely, with the family name of "elephant" its arms do not involve the animal. However during the 16th century a unique form of painted ceiling became fashionable in Scotland. Rossend Castle in Fifeshire has a fine example, decorated with a variety of devices including the elephant & castle. These are thought to have been copied from the "Devises Heroïques of Claude Paradin", a book of fantastic beasts published in 1557 but whether they have any symbolic or heraldic significance is unclear. The ceiling also bears the initials "SRM" which are those of Sir Robert Melville which suggests it was painted sometime after 1580.[43]

A portion of the ceiling at Rossend

ELEFANTORDENEN

There has been no popular tradition of the elephant & castle in Europe as in this country but when the animal does occur it is associated with the most senior nobility. Elefantordenen is the highest order of Denmark. It has existed since 1693. The regalia consist of a chain of alternating elephants and castles. It is derived from the badge of a medieval confraternity called the Fellowship of the Mother of God which incorporated a collar of links in the form of elephants. Doubtless the elephant was derived from the ancient bestiary traditions. The confraternity was closed during the reformation but in 1699 Frederick IV, King of Denmark and Norway, incorporated the design in his coat of arms and the device is depicted on the ceiling of the Long Hall of Rosenborg Castle in Copenhagen.

KLEBERCZ

This was a noble Hungarian family. According to a family legend the founder of the dynasty was a member of an expedition to Sicily sent by the King of Hungary to seek the Sicilian princess' hand in marriage. He was given an elephant as a present which he took back to Hungary and presented to the King. In return he was rewarded with large estates. The village which he founded is still called Oliphaunt.

HELFENSTEIN

The House of Helfenstein was a German noble family which held the rank of Count and was very significant in the 13th and 14th centuries. The elephant is probably a pun or corruption of the name Helfenstein which is pronounced "elefanten". A more fanciful explanation is that the elephant is associated with the first ancestor of the family, by the name of Helfrich, a captain of a Roman Legion based in Germany, because this legion had fought against Hannibal four centuries earlier.

CORPORATE AND CIVIC ARMS

As already discussed, the elephant in the arms of the Cutlers' Company probably relates to the use of ivory. However, like the camel, it has also been adopted as an emblem of commerce especially in connection with Africa and India.

THE COMPANY OF ROYAL ADVENTURERS TRADING TO AFRICA

This was a slaving company set up in 1662 by the Stuart family in partnership with a group of London merchants. It was granted a monopoly over the English slave trade and established a string of forts on the west Coast of Africa. Between 1672 and 1689 it transported around 100,000 slaves and its profits made a major contribution to the financial power of the City of London. After much opposition from rival groups of merchants, like Bristol's "Society of Merchant Venturers", Parliament repealed the monopoly in 1698. The Company continued slaving until 1731 when it abandoned the trade in favour of importing ivory and gold. The Company's arms depicted an elephant & castle. From 1668 to 1722 the Company provided gold to the English Mint. Coins made with this gold bear an elephant or elephant & castle below the bust of the monarch. This gold also gave the coinage its name, the "guinea" after its region of origin.

James II
1686

William &
Mary
1693

38

THE COMPANY OF SCOTLAND TRADING
TO AFRICA AND THE INDIES

The arms granted to Inverness burgh in 1900 have an elephant and a camel as supporters (above left). Inverness was an important trading town and the animals were adopted from the arms of "The Company of Scotland Trading to Africa and the Indies" (above right). This was established by Act of the Scots Parliament in 1695 to avoid the monopoly that had been granted to the Honorable East India Company by Elizabeth I. The collapse of the "Darien Adventure", Scotland's attempt to establish a trading colony in Darien, now part of Panama, was a major factor in the Scottish Parliament's acceptance of the Act of Union in 1707. The company's arms show the modes of transport: a ship, a camel and a pack horse. The elephant & castle represents trade. The Royal Bank of Scotland grew out of the failure of the colony, as its origins lie in the banking ambitions of the Commissioners of 'the Equivalent' – the sum awarded to Scotland under the Union in compensation for the losses incurred at Darien. As a result the archive collections of RBS include many papers relating to the Darien Adventure.

THE PENINSULAR & ORIENTAL
STEAM COMPANY

Now known as just as P&O, the company was granted these arms in 1937 its centenary year. The company is now much diversified but its original trade was supplying sea routes to the dominions. The animals on the shield represent India, Australia and Hong Kong. The style of the castle on the elephant suggests that it was modelled on the famous elephant & castle of Newington.

LONDON BOROUGH OF CAMDEN

The arms of the borough provide an interesting example of heraldic evolution by amalgamation. They contain elements from the former Boroughs of Hampstead, Holborn and St Pancras. The elephant is derived from the arms of St. Pancras which were based on those of Charles Pratt, 1st Earl Camden (1830 – 1891) who owned the land on which Camden town was developed.

Camden   St Pancras   Charles Pratt

BOLTON BOROUGH COUNCIL

There is an official stamp belonging to the Clerk of the Board of Trustees bearing an elephant & castle that dates from 1799 but the arms were only incorporated in 1890. The crest of an elephant & castle represents the connection with the old county of Coventry. Bolton is very proud of its elephant and there are examples of the animal all over the town. Although the official arms depict an elephant with a tower after the style of Coventry, curiously many of the examples around the town bear castles in the style of the Cutlers which probably reflects the influence of the Newington emblem.

Left: Crest from the Arms of Bolton Borough Council
Right: Memorial plaque on a bridge dated 1902

DUNBARTONSHIRE

The elephant & castle depicted here is from the arms of the Royal Burgh of Dumbarton. An elephant seems an improbable device for a medieval Scottish Burgh. It is said to have been chosen because the animal's shape resembled Dumbarton Rock and the castle represents Dumbarton Castle. Its earliest appearance is in 1357 on the seal of a document relating to the ransom of the Scottish King David II. In 1787 the poet Robert Burns visited Dumbarton and the magistrates presented him with this Burgess Ticket which depicts the old Burgh arms. Burns' signature can be seen at the bottom.

ALLERDALE BOROUGH

Here is an example of the continuing popularity of the elephant & castle icon. Allerdale was formed by the amalgamation of several metropolitan districts in Cumbria and was granted Borough status in 1995. Soon

afterwards it achieved this amazing coat of arms. The crest bears an elephant with a castle holding a miner's pick in its trunk and is surmounted by a weather vane. The arms were designed so that every single feature symbolises some aspect of the history and culture of areas within the borough.

BADGES AND BRANDS

The Carthaginian General Hannibal is famous for marching with 2000 war elephants over the Alps in 218 BC. By the time of Claudius' invasion of Britain, due to changes in tactics and scarcity of the animals, the use of war elephants in Europe was almost at an end. Claudius used only small numbers of the animals and this was their last significant use in battle. In India and Asia elephants continued to be used in warfare until recent times. In both the Second World War and the Vietnam war large numbers of elephants were used as transports and there were tragic incidents where the allies engaged in bombing these animals.[44]

Left: S*hips badge of HMS Coventry*

Right: Collar dogs of the Duke of Wellington's Regiment

There were three of ships of the Royal Navy named HMS Elephant during the 18th century. The aircraft carrier HMS Hermes, which was the flagship during the Falklands war, was originally laid down as HMS Elephant but construction was suspended in 1945 and when the modified design was completed in 1957 the name was changed to HMS Hermes. Six ships of the Royal Navy have been named HMS Coventry. The first was a 48 gun ship of the line launched in 1695. The last was a Type 42 (Sheffield Class) destroyer which was sunk during the Falklands War. The ship's badge was introduced in the navy when figureheads went out of use. The badge of HMS Coventry, illustrated here, is taken from the arms of Coventry City.

The elephant is associated with regiments that have connections with India or Asia. The Duke of Wellington's Regiment had an Indian elephant with a houda as its mascot and this was worn as a collar dog or badge. The 19th Royal Hussars Cavalry Regiment also had a badge with an Indian elephant. Both these regiments were originally raised by the Honorable East India Company for service in India. The 4th County of London Yeomanry was formed as a regiment for British overseas volunteers in England with four Colonial Squadrons.

'A' Squadron, known as British Asian, had a cap badge of an elephant. The cap badge of the Royal Dublin Fusiliers had a very unusual combination of a leopard above an elephant. The badge of the Gurkha Rifles is an elephant with a castle. The picture below is from the Gurkha Memorial in Winchester Cathedral.

27 Squadron RAF was formed in 1915 equipped with Martinsyde Elephant fighter aircraft. The squadron also had a long period of service in India. The squadron is still operational and flies helicopters. In 2012 the Squadron was presented with a baby elephant as a mascot.

The new London Adelphi building was opened in 1938 and is now considered one of the finest examples of Art Deco architecture in London. It is decorated with Portland stone vignettes by Jacob Epstein. The building was a speculative development and Epstein may have been hedging his bets in the design of its decorations however the general theme represents labour and industry. There is a winged Mercury over the entrance while the frieze around the building includes panels depicting cornucopia, pestle and mortar and elephant & castle.

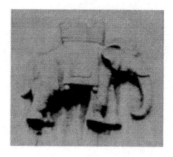

Gurkha Rifles   27 Squadron RAF   Adelphi Building

The "Elephant & Castle" is a traditional name for hostelries in England. Religious symbolism was once common in the names of inns and taverns but decreased after Henry VIII's break from Rome. However some examples of these medieval names survive in corrupted form such as "Goat and Compass" and "Hope & Anchor". The "Elephant & Castle" may belong to this category as a corruption of Infanta de Castile. Some inns of that name may well predate the Elephant & Castle of Newington but it is surely the circumstances surrounding that particular hostelry that have led to the name's contemporary popularity and it can now be found throughout the English-speaking world. The Elephant & Castle Pub and Restaurants Company has a chain of venues across North America. Its sign is almost an exact copy of the Newington elephant but some signs show 'interesting variations on the theme such as the one below from the Elephant & Castle restaurant in New York. London was once famous for its tobacco blending trade. The firm of C.E. McConnell produced a brand called "Elephant & Castle". High quality smoking mixtures were exported all over the world and this brand would also have helped to carry the name to many parts.

TAIL PIECE

The Noble Game of Elephant & Castle was published in 1822. It was a race game played on a magnificently coloured board depicting an elephant with a houda and an Indian driver or mahout taking the players on a Grand Tour from the frozen wastes of Northern Russia to India and the Far East. On the way it describes the customs and appearance of the people, outrageously comparing their way of life to that of the civilised  British. The game is a reflection on both Victorian pride of Empire and the continuing popularity of the icon.

SOURCES & NOTES

1. Humphrey, Stephen *Elephant and Castle a History* (2013)
2. Welch, Charles *History of the Cutlers' Company Vol. I*, (1916)
3. College of Arms, website
4. Harleian Society Vol.1 *Visitation of London 1568*, (1869)
   Harleian Society Vol.109 *Visitation of London* (1963)
5. College of Arms (private communication)
6. Welch, Charles *Coat Armour of the London Livery Companies*
7. Fraters, G H *The Complete Golden Dawn System of Magic*, (1984)
8. Jan Kochanowski *"Ches"* published in 1565
9. Haskins, Charles *The Ancient Trade Guilds and Companies of Salisbury* (1910)
10. Lloyd, G I H *The Cutlery Trades* (1913)
11. *Wiltshire County Mirror and Express, July 1897*
12. Du Garde Peach, L *The Company of Cutlers in Hallamshire in the County of York* (1960)
13. Fairbank, William surveyor 1806;
    (Private communication (localstudies.library@sheffield.gov.uk)
14. Walford, E *Old and New London* Vol.VI (1897)
15. Southwark and Lambeth Archaeological Society
    (private communication)
16. Stow, John, *Survey of the Cities of London & Westminster* (1598)
17. Timbs, John *Romance of London* (1865)
18. Morton, H V *In Search of London* (1951)
19. Fraser, Antonia (ed.) *The Lives of the Kings & and Queens of England* (1998)
20. Druce, George C *The Elephant in Medieval Legend and Art.* Journal of the Royal Archaeological Institute, (1919)
21. Henderson, Arnold *C Development of Medieval Fable and Bestiary,* (Berkeley University, 1973)
22. Druce, George C *Animals in English wood carvings* Walpole Society, London (1913)
23. Sands, H *Extracts from the documentary History of the Tower of London* Royal Archaeological Institute Volume LXIX, (1912)
24. Fiore Dei Liberi *Il Fior Di Battaglia (The Flower of the Battle)* (MS circa 1409)
25. *British Library Harley MS 6149*
26. Perry, Guy, *John of Brienne, King of Jerusalem, Emperor of Constantinople,* (2013)

27. Powell Siddons, M *Hearldic Badges in England & Wales* (2009)
28. Goodall, John *Waller's Series of Monumental Brasses,*
29. Strickland, Agnes *Lives of the Queens of England Vol. 1* (1840)
30. Lord Beaumont was designated as "the King's kinsman " in 1 Edw.II.,
31. Skillington, S H *Beaumanor & its Lords & their Connections* Leics Arch. Soc. (1946)
32. Nichols, John Gough *The Armorial Windows of Woodhouse Chapel* Leics. Architect. and Archaeol. Soc. (1860)
33. Harleian Society Vol.62. *Visitation of the County of Warwick in the Year 1682-1683* (1877)
34. Dormer Harris, Mary D *Life in an Old English Town*, (1898)
35. Elkiss, T H *The Quest for an African Eldorado: Southern Zambezia, and the Portuguese, 1500-1865* (1981)
36. Burke, Sir John Bernard *The General Armory* (1848)
37. The Victorian artist's rendering of the inscription appears to refer to Edward I but it actually reads reads *"Edwardi reg Angl an greogn debitor apd Covetre"* and is typical of the seals of the period for debtors bonds.
38. Jones, Alfred E *Memorials of Old North Wales* (1913)
39. Lloyd-Hughes, D G *Pwllheli An old Welsh Town and its History*
40. Heseltine, Peter *A Bestiary of Brass*. (2006)
41. Burke, Sir John Bernard *The General Armory*
42. Harleian Society Vol.5 *Visitations of the County of Oxford*
43. Apted, M R and Robertson, W *Proceedings of the Society of Antiquarians of Scotland vol. 104*
44. Kistler, John *Animals in the Military*: (2011)

ILLUSTRATIONS

The images on pages plate i are owned by the Cutlers Company. Images on plates ii-v are used with permission of the College of Arms of London. Images from Cutlers' Hall in Sheffield on plate vi are used with permission of the Company of Cutlers in Hallamshire. All other images are used with permission or are in the public domain because copyright has expired or they are used under the terms of the GNU Free Documentation Licence.